THE NBA

A HISTORY OF HOOPS

Published by Creative Education
P.O. Box 227, Mankato, Minnesota 56002
Creative Education is an imprint of The Creative Company
www.thecreativecompany.us

Design and production by Christine Vanderbeek
Art direction by Rita Marshall

Printed by Corporate Graphics in the United States of America

Photographs by Corbis (Bettmann), Dreamstime (Munktcu), Getty Images
(Andrew D. Bernstein/NBAE, Garrett W. Ellwood/NBAE, Mitchell Funk,
Jesse D. Garrabrant/NBAE, Walter Iooss Jr./Sports Illustrated, George
Long/Sports Illustrated, Melissa Majchrzak/NBAE, NBAPhotos/NBAE,
Hy Peskin/Sports Illustrated, Christian Petersen, Dick Raphael/NBAE,
SM/AIUEO, Kent Smith/NBAE, Justin Sullivan, Visions Of Our Land,
Rocky Widner/NBAE), iStockphoto (Brandon Laufenberg)

Library of Congress Cataloging-in-Publication Data
Omoth, Tyler.
The story of the Golden State Warriors / by Tyler Omoth.
p. cm. — (The NBA: a history of hoops)
Includes index.
Summary: The history of the Golden State Warriors professional
basketball team from its start in Philadelphia, Pennsylvania, in 1946
to today, spotlighting the franchise's greatest players and moments.
ISBN 978-1-58341-944-1
1. Golden State Warriors (Basketball team)—History—Juvenile literature.
I. Title. II. Series.
GV885.52.G64O46 2010   796.323'640979461—dc22   2009035025

CPSIA: 120109 PO1093

First Edition
2 4 6 8 9 7 5 3 1

Page 3: Guard Jamal Crawford
Pages 4–5: Center Andris Biedrins

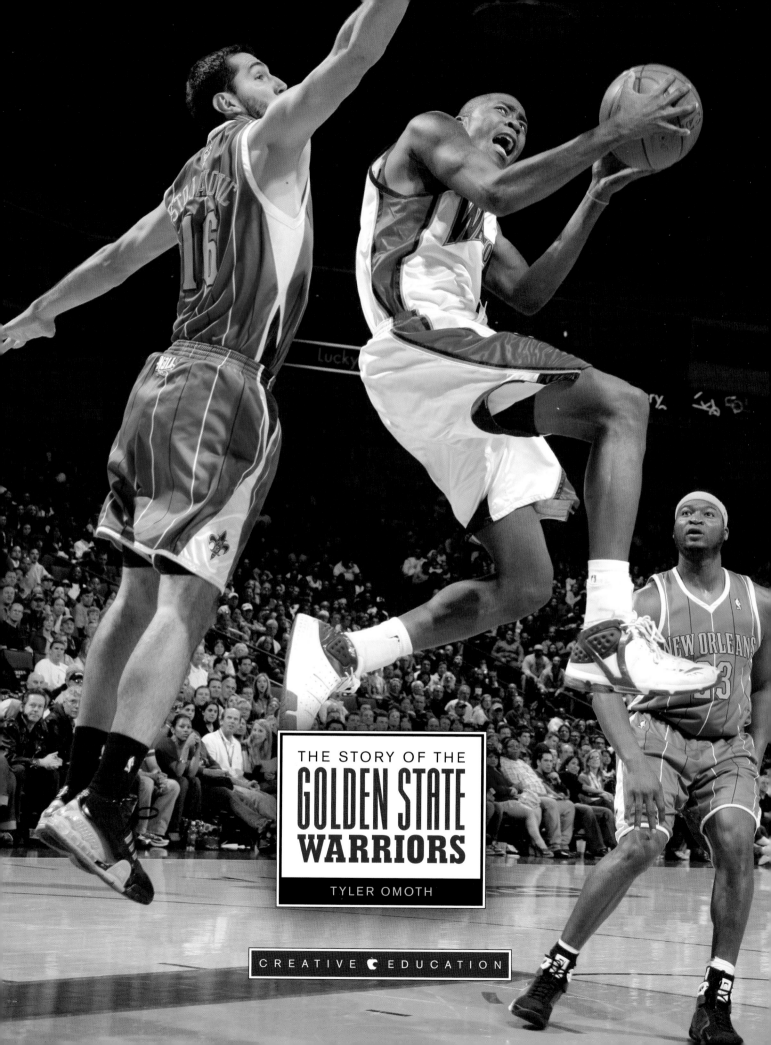

THE STORY OF THE
GOLDEN STATE
WARRIORS

TYLER OMOTH

CREATIVE ● EDUCATION

CONTENTS

CHAPTER ONE

EAST COAST ORIGINS

In 1848, a sawmill operator named James Wilson Marshall found gold in California. His discovery sparked the hopes and imaginations of settlers throughout America and led to a feverish migration from the eastern states by people of all walks of life looking to strike it rich. The gold rush led to rapid growth in the Bay Area of California. Small settlements such as San Francisco and Oakland quickly grew to become centers of commerce and destinations for people eager to take a chance at finding a new, more comfortable life through West Coast gold.

More than a century later, a similar storyline played out when a professional basketball team called the Warriors was struggling to survive on the East Coast. The Warriors, who initially made their home in Philadelphia, Pennsylvania, made like the gold seekers of the 1800s and looked for brighter prospects by moving west to California in 1962. Since then, the Bay cities of San Francisco and Oakland have shared a National Basketball Association (NBA) team with a rich tradition, a franchise that is appropriately known as the Golden State Warriors.

San Francisco's most famous landmark is its gargantuan Golden Gate Bridge, which has helped to frame views of the city since 1937.

W hen the first major professional basketball league—the Basketball Association of America (BAA)—was formed in 1946, it started out with 11 teams, including the Warriors of Philadelphia. Basketball pioneer Edward Gottlieb founded the franchise and also served as the Warriors' first coach. He got the team off to an excellent start by signing a dynamic forward from Kentucky named Joe Fulks, who led the league in scoring in 1946–47 with 23.2 points per game. "He made one-handed shots, jump shots, right-handed [and] left-handed set shots from a distance, driving shots, hooks with his right or left hand," said Gottlieb. "He was also basketball's first jump shooter."

Led by the scoring of "Jumpin' Joe" and guard Tony Musi, and the steady assists of forward Howie Dallmar, the Warriors won the first BAA championship in 1947 in a four-games-to-one series rout of the Chicago Stags. Philadelphia made it to the league finals again in 1948 but came up short against the Baltimore Bullets. The Warriors' third—and last— season in the BAA was a losing one, as they could muster only a 28–32 record. The BAA and its rival, the National Basketball League (NBL), then merged to form the NBA in 1949, with 17 teams, including the Warriors, as inaugural members.

IT'S ALWAYS BEST TO MAKE A GOOD FIRST IMPRESSION, AND THAT'S JUST WHAT THE WARRIORS DID WHEN THEY WON THE BASKETBALL ASSOCIATION OF AMERICA'S VERY FIRST LEAGUE CHAMPIONSHIP. The BAA started up in 1946 with 11 teams, including the newly created Philadelphia Warriors. The players on the Warriors' roster had little to no experience playing professional basketball, but in the newly formed league, they didn't need a lot. "Jumpin' Joe" Fulks, a 25-year-old rookie forward out of Murray State University, led the league in scoring with 23.2 points per game; his total of 1,389 points was nearly one-third of the total points scored by the Warriors all season. After finishing second in the Eastern Division with a 35–25 record, Philadelphia defeated the St. Louis Bombers in the first round of the playoffs. They then trounced the New York Knickerbockers in the second round to advance to the first-ever BAA Finals, where they rolled over the Chicago Stags, four games to one. In winning the inaugural BAA title, the team that became today's Golden State Warriors got off to the perfect start.

ife in the NBA was a struggle for the Warriors at first. After another losing season, the Warriors bounced back in 1950–51 to capture the top spot in the Eastern Division with a 40–26 record, but they were knocked out in the first round of the playoffs. In 1952–53, the Warriors plummeted to 12–57. Luckily, two new arrivals, guard Paul Arizin and high-scoring center Neil Johnston, were on the scene to help new coach George Senesky take the team back to the top. Philadelphia catapulted to a 45–27 record in 1955–56, then captured its first NBA championship, beating the Fort Wayne Pistons four games to one in front of record crowds.

After winning the 1956 championship, Philadelphia discovered that talent had improved around the league, and the Warriors were no longer top dogs. Despite solid play from Arizin and forward Joe Graboski, the team came up short in the playoffs the next two seasons and fell to 32–40 in 1958–59. As the competition in the NBA got stiffer, the Warriors found themselves in need of a player who could separate them from the pack once again.

Marksman Neil Johnston was a 1950s scoring machine, leading all NBA players in points for three straight seasons (1952–53 to 1954–55).

CHAPTER TWO

WILT'S WARRIORS

In 1955, the NBA added a new rule allowing teams to exhange their first-round pick in the league's annual draft for the right to claim any local college player in hopes of keeping homegrown talent close to their fans. The Warriors took advantage of this rule in 1959 and snatched up 7-foot-1 and 250-pound Philadelphia native Wilt Chamberlain as their "territorial" selection in that year's NBA Draft. "He could do whatever he wanted to do on a basketball court," Warriors coach Frank McGuire said of the talented center. "No player, not even Bill Russell, could stop him."

Wilt Chamberlain burst onto the NBA scene like no other, averaging an incredible 37.6 points and 27 boards per game in his first season.

B ill Russell, the great defensive center for the Boston Celtics, couldn't exactly stop Chamberlain, but his Celtics teams repeatedly came out on top, as they would win 9 of the 10 NBA championships in the 1960s. During those years, Chamberlain and Russell frequently clashed with physical battles on both ends of the floor in what was quite possibly the NBA's best rivalry ever at the center position.

Six years of not making it to the NBA Finals, and another heart-breaking loss to the Celtics in the 1962 Eastern Division finals, proved to be too much for Philadelphia fans. Attendance waned, Gottlieb sold the Warriors to a group of San Francisco investors, and the Warriors headed west to play at their new home, San Francisco's Cow Palace. Chamberlain continued to dominate on the West Coast, leading the NBA in scoring for the fourth straight year, but the 1962–63 San Francisco Warriors finished a mere 31–49.

In 1963, Alex Hannum was hired as San Francisco's head coach. Hannum knew his team had talent. Guards Guy Rodgers and the intense Al Attles formed a solid backcourt, and young and aggressive center/forward Nate Thurmond played a big role as a rebounder and shot blocker. But the coach depended mainly on his star center. "For us to win," Hannum explained, "Wilt has to play like Bill Russell when we're on defense and play like Wilt Chamberlain when we're on offense."

The Warriors powered their way to the 1964 NBA Finals behind the dominance of Chamberlain and the hot shooting of forward Tom Meschery, who averaged 16.8 points per game during the team's playoff run. However, the Warriors fell to the mighty Celtics once again, four games to one. After San Francisco got off to a poor start the next season, the Warriors traded Chamberlain back to Philadelphia, where a new NBA team—the 76ers—had developed from the relocation of the former Syracuse Nationals. For all his record-setting years with the Warriors, Chamberlain never had managed to bring the franchise a championship trophy.

The Chamberlain trade allowed two new stars to rise in San Francisco. The first was Thurmond, who quickly evolved into one of the NBA's best centers. The other was forward Rick Barry, who joined the Warriors as a frail-looking youngster in 1965. Over the next few seasons, Barry would prove capable of scoring almost at will from anywhere on the court, and his deadeye shooting would earn him the nickname "The Golden Gunner."

INTRODUCING...

WILT CHAMBERLAIN

POSITION CENTER
HEIGHT 7-FOOT-1
WARRIORS SEASONS 1959–65

HE WAS BIG, DOMINANT, AND POSSIBLY THE BEST PLAYER EVER TO PLAY THE GAME OF BASKETBALL. The NBA record book is littered with his name. He scored the most points ever in a single game with a whopping 100-point effort versus the New York Knicks in 1962. He pulled down 55 rebounds in one 1960 game, which is also tops all time. Furthermore, he's the only center ever to have led the league in assists (during the 1967–68 season). Wilt "The Stilt" Chamberlain stood 7-foot-1, and despite his lean build, he was both powerful and athletic. Opposing teams frequently tried to double- or even triple-team Chamberlain to stop him, but his size and strength allowed him to play through those tactics and still dominate. When he retired in 1973, he was the all-time NBA scoring leader, and he still holds the league mark for most career rebounds with 23,924. Chamberlain's greatest adversary was Celtics center Bill Russell, who tipped his cap to Chamberlain, saying, "Wilt was the greatest offensive player I have ever seen." The record books agree.

NATE THURMOND WAS A BIG GUY WHO COULD DO IT ALL. Thurmond followed the great Wilt Chamberlain as a star center for the Warriors, and while he wasn't as flashy as his predecessor, he was arguably more versatile than Chamberlain. Opponents had to beware of Thurmond down low, because he was a fierce defender who excelled at both blocking shots and snatching rebounds. As he gained experience, he also became an offensive force, which made him one of the game's greatest all-around players. On October 18, 1974, as a member of the Chicago Bulls, he became the first NBA player ever to record a "quadruple-double" (notching double-digit totals in 4 statistical categories), with 22 points, 14 rebounds, 13 assists, and 12 blocks in one game. Especially on defense, Thurmond had few peers. "His statistics aren't overwhelming, but his presence on the court is unbelievable," said Warriors guard Walt Hazzard. "As for blocking shots, I've seen guys get offensive rebounds and then go back 15 feet to make sure they can get a shot off. They know Nate is there."

INTRODUCING...

NATE THURMOND

POSITION CENTER / FORWARD
HEIGHT 6-FOOT-11
WARRIORS SEASONS 1963–74

ed by Barry and Thurmond, the 1966–67 Warriors again reached the NBA Finals, where they faced off against the 76ers and their old teammate, Chamberlain. Barry poured in an average of 41 points per game in the Finals, but the Warriors couldn't stand up to Philadelphia's powerful inside attack, and the 76ers prevailed in six games.

The next season, Barry left to join a team in the new American Basketball Association (ABA), and Thurmond assumed the spotlight mostly by himself. Powered by a low-post offense that revolved around Thurmond and forward Rudy LaRusso, who had a career season with 21.8 points per game, the Warriors made it to the Western Division finals before losing to the Los Angeles Lakers in a four-game sweep.

CHAPTER THREE

BATTLING TO THE TOP

After San Francisco made early exits from the playoffs in 1968 and 1969, Al Attles took over as a player/coach with 30 games remaining in the 1969–70 season. Shortly after getting a new coach, the franchise got a revised image. Since arriving in the Bay Area, the team had played home games in three different cities—San Francisco, Oakland, and San Jose. Finally, in 1971, the team settled into the Oakland Coliseum Arena and dropped its exclusive San Francisco affiliation in favor of a name that it hoped would broaden its fan base, becoming the Golden State Warriors.

The renamed and resettled Warriors were a team with some talent. Thurmond anchored the inside along with forward Jerry Lucas, while guard Jeff Mullins paced the Warriors in scoring. In 1972, the Warriors' Golden Gunner returned as Rick Barry came back from the ABA for a second stint in Warriors gold and blue. Still, the Warriors of the early '70s were successful in the regular season but sputtered in the playoffs.

Jeff Mullins spent 10 seasons with the Warriors, earning trips to the 1969, 1970, and 1971 NBA All-Star Games with his pinpoint shooting.

The 1974–75 season changed all that. Before the season, Thurmond was traded to the Chicago Bulls for center Clifford Ray, a defensive specialist. The Warriors then added guards Charles Johnson and Butch Beard and smooth rookie forward Jamaal Wilkes to the starting lineup. With Coach Attles preaching a fast-break offense and a gambling defense, the Warriors fought their way to a 48–34 record.

Although their record was not phenomenal, the Warriors headed into the 1975 playoffs with confidence, and in the first two rounds, they toppled the Seattle SuperSonics and the Bulls to reach the NBA Finals. Golden State faced the heavily favored Washington Bullets in the championship round, but in a stunning upset, the Warriors swept the series in four straight games to win the title. "We cared about winning and did whatever we could to win," said Barry. "It was an atmosphere you'd like to see more professional teams have. I defy anyone to find anything like it."

DODGING THE BULLETS

Rick Barry takes a long shot versus the Bullets in the 1975 NBA Finals.

EVERYONE LOVES AN UNDERDOG, SO WHEN THE WARRIORS MADE IT ALL THE WAY TO THE 1975 NBA FINALS TO FACE THE WASHINGTON BULLETS, THEY HAD TO BE FEELING THE LOVE. For most of the season, NBA fans had focused on the battle in the Eastern Conference between the Bullets and the Celtics. The two powerhouses had each posted a superb 60–22 record, while the Warriors had finished with a respectable, but certainly not intimidating, 48–34 mark. When playoff time arrived, the Warriors were playing their best ball and fought through the first two rounds of the playoffs to square off against the heavily favored Bullets, who featured such stars as guard Kevin Porter and forward Elvin Hayes. Every game was intense, but the Warriors stunned the Bullets with smothering team defense and clutch scoring by Rick Barry to pick up three straight victories. In Game 4, the Warriors fell behind but were able to scratch their way back to win 96–95. The Finals Most Valuable Player (MVP) award went to Barry, who still claims, "It has to be the greatest upset in the history of the NBA."

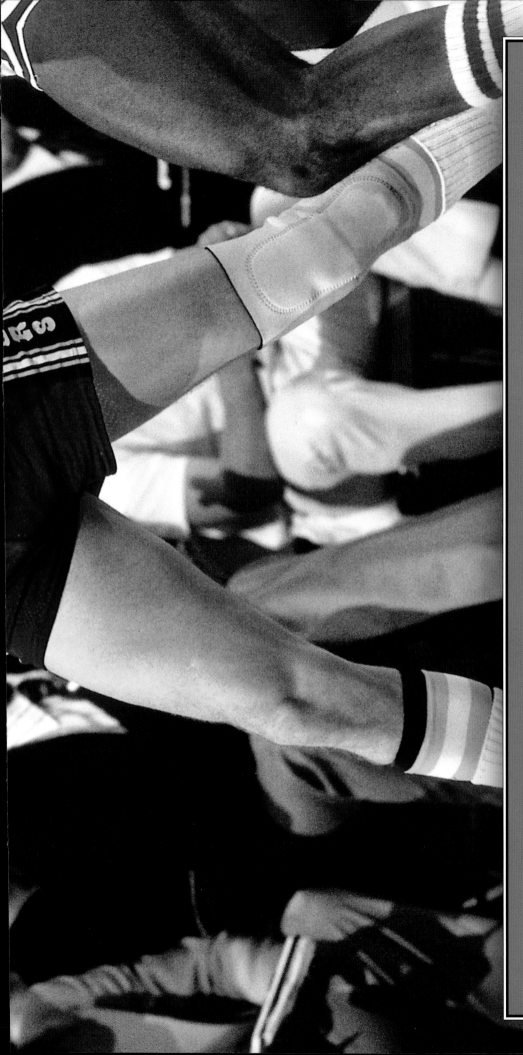

ONE WOULDN'T EXPECT AN NBA PLAYER WHO his own teammates as he pushed everyone around him He led the league in free-throw percentage six times in

USES A GRANNY SHOT TO SHOOT HIS FREE to the limits, but there was no question he played to his career and finished his NBA career as a 90 percent

THROWS TO BE AN INTIMIDATING FORCE ON THE win. With a sharp outside shot and a knack for cutting free-throw shooter—second-best in league history. "He's

COURT, BUT THAT'S JUST WHAT RICK BARRY WAS through the lane to either score a layup or earn two an intense competitor, whether it's basketball, golf,

THROUGHOUT HIS CAREER. Barry was a fierce foul shots, Barry was one of the most prolific scorers in checkers, or anything else," said Warriors coach Bill

competitor who wanted to win at all costs. His intensity NBA history. In 1974–75, he averaged 30.6 points per Sharman. "He just doesn't want to lose."

sometimes got on the nerves of his opponents and even game to lead the Warriors to an NBA championship.

he next season, Barry, Wilkes, and swingman Phil Smith powered the Warriors to a 59–23 record—an all-time franchise best. But the team couldn't get past the Phoenix Suns in the Western Conference finals. After losing in the second round the next year to the Lakers, the Warriors entered into the bleakest stretch in franchise history, missing the playoffs every year from 1977–78 through 1985–86.

Still, the Warriors teams of the early 1980s were not without stars. Young center Robert Parish was beginning to flourish before the Warriors dealt him to the Celtics in 1980 for two draft picks. Golden State used one of those picks to select center Joe Barry Carroll, who put up 6 seasons of at least 17 points per game for the Warriors. The trade would haunt Warriors fans, though, as they watched Parish go on to be a major part of three NBA championships with the Celtics. Explosive forward Bernard King and charismatic guard World B. Free stepped into the spotlight during the 1981–82 season and helped the Warriors to a 45–37 record, but the team missed the playoffs by a single game.

THE GRANNY SHOT

Wilt Chamberlain puts up a free throw granny-shot style.

IT'S HOW MOST LITTLE KIDS FIRST SHOOT A BASKETBALL AND HOW AN OLD LADY WOULD PROBABLY LET THE BALL FLY. The famous "granny shot" in basketball involves holding the ball with both hands below one's waist, bending at the knees, and throwing the ball upward in an underhand motion. It's simple, but it looks rather silly. It's not a shot one would expect to see in an NBA game, but two Warriors stars found it a worthwhile technique at the free-throw line. Wilt Chamberlain, a center who struggled mightily to make free throws, tried the granny shot, but he didn't stick with it for long. Rick Barry, a slick-shooting forward of the 1970s, on the other hand, used it almost exclusively when he stepped to the "charity stripe." The Hall-of-Famer was a 90 percent career free-throw shooter using the granny style. "I didn't [originally] want any part of it, but my father drove me nuts until I tried it," Barry said. "And amazingly, it worked. Nobody ever teased me, but it's hard to tease somebody when the ball keeps going in."

AS A PLAYER, AL ATTLES WAS NICKNAMED "THE DESTROYER." He was never the fastest or most athletic player on his team, but he was a tenacious defender and a rugged enforcer who was feared throughout the league for his temper and physical play. When he became the Warriors' head coach, he showed off his strength as a strategist. He liked his teams to be fast and in remarkable shape so they could wear out their opponents. Hired in 1969, Attles was one of the first African American coaches in the NBA, and his battle with the Bullets and their coach, K. C. Jones, in the 1975 Finals was pro basketball's first championship matchup between two black head coaches. Attles did not play favorites as coach and would frequently use his lesser-known players as much as his stars if he felt it would help him win a game, and his teams tirelessly attacked their opponents on each end of the court. "That's really where the team took on Al's personality," said Warriors forward Jamaal Wilkes. "We were quick, we were tough, and we challenged people."

INTRODUCING...

AL ATTLES

POSITION GUARD, COACH
HEIGHT 6 FEET
WARRIORS SEASONS
AS PLAYER 1960–71
AS COACH 1969–83

The next season, King left for greener pastures in New York, and an injured Warriors lineup stumbled to a 30–52 finish. Despite consistent scoring from shooting guard Terry Teagle, Golden State finished with losing records in each of the next three seasons before new ownership and a new coach arrived in 1986. It was then that radio mogul Franklin Mieuli, who had owned the team since its relocation to California, sold it to an ownership group led by business entrepreneurs Jim Fitzgerald and Dan Finnane. The new owners wasted little time in making changes, naming George Karl the new head coach before the next season.

The move paid off, as the Warriors made the playoffs for the first time in nearly a decade with a 42–40 mark. After sneaking past the Utah Jazz in a hard-fought, five-game series, Golden State came up short against the Lakers, losing four games to one. The 1987–88 season was a big step backward, as the team could muster only a 20–62 record. Coach Karl resigned late in the season, and Don Nelson took up the clipboard as coach and general manager.

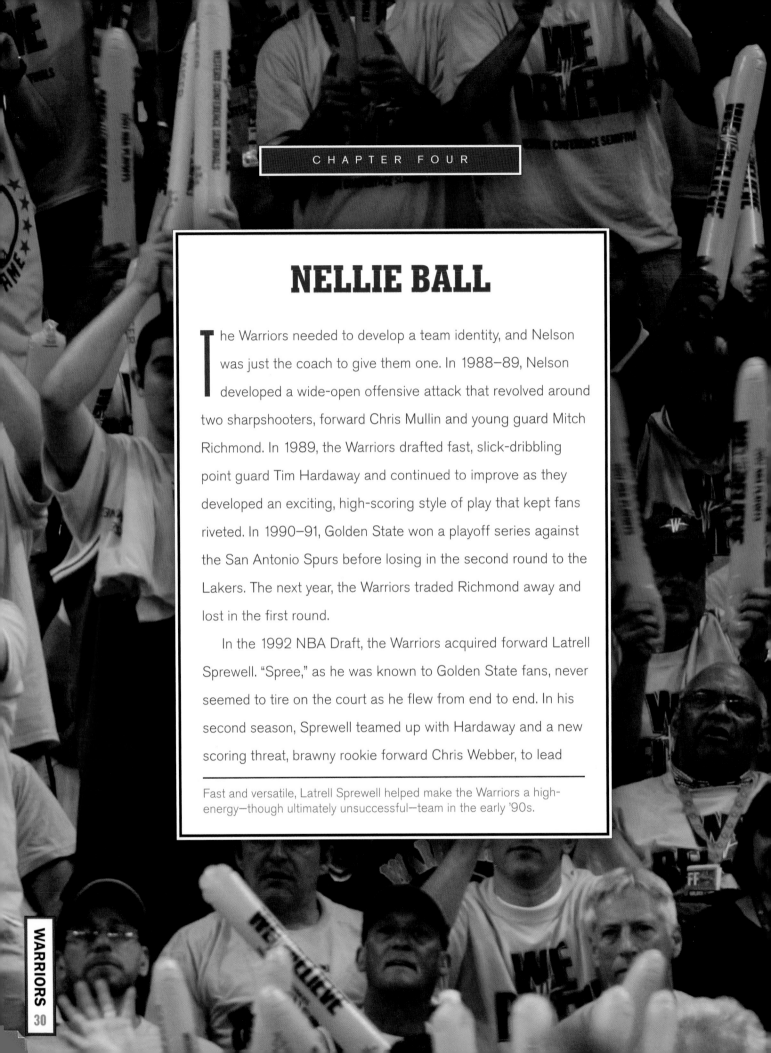

CHAPTER FOUR

NELLIE BALL

The Warriors needed to develop a team identity, and Nelson was just the coach to give them one. In 1988–89, Nelson developed a wide-open offensive attack that revolved around two sharpshooters, forward Chris Mullin and young guard Mitch Richmond. In 1989, the Warriors drafted fast, slick-dribbling point guard Tim Hardaway and continued to improve as they developed an exciting, high-scoring style of play that kept fans riveted. In 1990–91, Golden State won a playoff series against the San Antonio Spurs before losing in the second round to the Lakers. The next year, the Warriors traded Richmond away and lost in the first round.

In the 1992 NBA Draft, the Warriors acquired forward Latrell Sprewell. "Spree," as he was known to Golden State fans, never seemed to tire on the court as he flew from end to end. In his second season, Sprewell teamed up with Hardaway and a new scoring threat, brawny rookie forward Chris Webber, to lead

Fast and versatile, Latrell Sprewell helped make the Warriors a high-energy—though ultimately unsuccessful—team in the early '90s.

the Warriors to a 50–32 record and a playoff berth. The Warriors were unable to get past Phoenix in the first round, though, as star forward Charles Barkley and the Suns swept Golden State in three straight games.

Unfortunately, just when it looked like Golden State was approaching true contender status, things fell apart. Coaches and players feuded, and in 1994, Webber was traded to the Bullets, and Nelson stepped down. By the end of the 1994–95 season, the Warriors were 26–56, and after Hardaway was traded away, only Sprewell remained as a star.

After two more losing seasons, the Warriors brought in new head coach P. J. Carlesimo in 1997. Soon after, during a practice, Carlesimo and the temperamental Sprewell got into an argument, and the All-Star guard physically attacked the coach. Sprewell never played for the Warriors again, drawing a one-year suspension from the NBA before being traded. Although he admitted threatening his coach's life, Sprewell was as brash in leaving town as he had been in arriving. "I made a mistake, and I'm sorry for that, but that doesn't make me a bad man," he said.

RUN T.M.C.

Mitch Richmond penetrates the defense with a drive.

IN THE MID-1980S, A THREE-MAN HIP-HOP GROUP CALLED RUN D.M.C. SHOOK UP THE MUSIC INDUSTRY WITH HITS SUCH AS "WALK THIS WAY" AND "YOU BE ILLIN'." Several years later, in the early '90s, the Warriors had their own super-trio shaking things up on the basketball court. With a high-octane offense, the Warriors were led by three very different stars who quickly became known around the league as "Run T.M.C." Tim Hardaway, Mitch Richmond, and Chris Mullin were the fuel that powered coach Don Nelson's "run-and-gun" offense. Hardaway was the lightning-quick ball handler, Richmond excelled at slashing to the basket, and Mullin played the role of outside sharpshooter. In 1990–91, all 3 players averaged more than 20 points per game in leading the team to a 44–38 record and a first-round playoff series win over San Antonio. Their combined 72.5 points-per-game average that season made them the highest-scoring trio in NBA history. Despite failing to make it to the NBA Finals, Run T.M.C. brought a new level of excitement to the Oakland Arena for Warriors fans.

EVERYONE LOVES A COMEBACK, AND CHRIS MULLIN'S EARLY CAREER WAS AN INSPIRING STORY FOR THE WARRIORS FAITHFUL AND BASKETBALL FANS THROUGHOUT THE COUNTRY. Picked seventh overall by the Warriors in the 1985 NBA Draft, Mullin was a scorer with unlimited potential, but he was also struggling with alcohol abuse. He proved to be a serviceable player in his first two years with the Warriors, but it wasn't until new coach Don Nelson urged him to seek treatment in 1987 that the Chris Mullin the Warriors had hoped for showed up. After his rehab, Mullin became a fitness fanatic and a tireless worker on and off the court. With a sweet left-handed jumper and outstanding fundamentals, he became a dynamic scorer and a perennial All-Star. Lacking top-level quickness, moves, or jumping ability, Mullin was one of the most unlikely stars in the NBA. In 1992, his marksmanship touch earned him a spot on the U.S. Olympic basketball team known as the "Dream Team." Teammate Tim Hardaway was among the many left in awe by Mullin's shooting accuracy. "You pass Mully the ball," Hardaway said, "and it's an assist."

INTRODUCING...

CHRIS MULLIN

POSITION FORWARD / GUARD
HEIGHT 6-FOOT-6
WARRIORS SEASONS 1985–97, 2000–01

The Sprewell incident cast a lingering cloud over the Warriors, and the team missed the playoffs each of the next eight seasons. Warriors management seemed to lack a clear rebuilding plan as players and coaches were shuffled like cards in and out of the franchise. One of the few bright spots in Golden State's lineup for several years was all-purpose forward Antawn Jamison, who joined the club through an NBA Draft trade in 1998.

Beginning in 2001, new faces began arriving to provide hope for the Warriors faithful. Explosive guard Jason Richardson and rugged forward Troy Murphy both joined the Warriors via the 2001 NBA Draft, and the team selected lanky forward Mike Dunleavy the following year. These three players formed a foundation in Golden State that would last for five years as they avoided the trades that had so often whisked the Warriors' best players away. The team still fell short of the playoffs the next three years, but the Warriors improved from a dismal 2000–01 season, in which they won only 17 games, to average 32 wins in each of the next 5 seasons.

TIM HARDAWAY'S GAME WAS A CLASSIC CASE OF "NOW YOU SEE HIM, NOW YOU DON'T." At only six feet tall, Hardaway was short by NBA standards, but he had energy and confidence to spare. His signature move was a crossover dribble in which he would fake a drive one direction, stop, and head the other way so fast that defenders would frequently fall over themselves trying to follow him. The only safe defense against Hardaway's crossover dribble was to back off far enough, but when that happened, he'd simply sink the outside shot. And when his team needed him the most, the little man with the big swagger was at his best. "When the game is on the line," said teammate Chris Mullin, "you have to wrestle him for the ball." Hardaway frequently took charge late in games for the Warriors with a variety of jumpers, aggressive drives, and fast-break buckets. "He's made more big plays, taken over more games, and led more runs than anybody we have," said Warriors coach Don Nelson. "When the hour is the bleakest, he saves the day. I think he's Mighty Mouse."

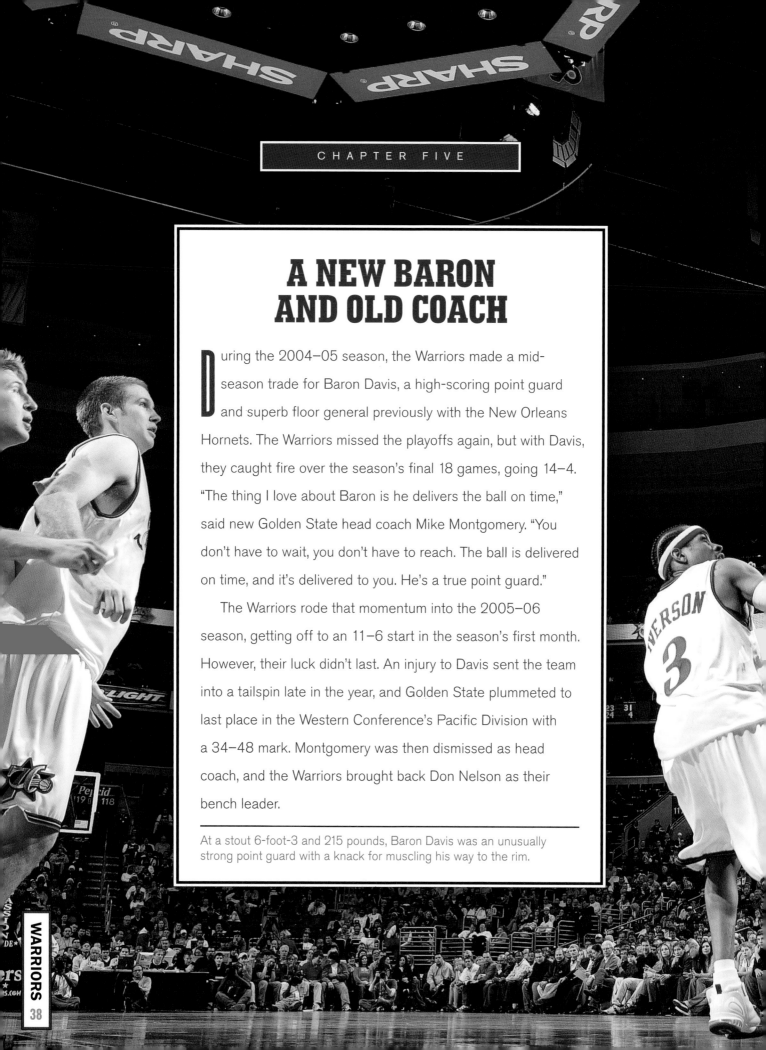

CHAPTER FIVE

A NEW BARON AND OLD COACH

During the 2004–05 season, the Warriors made a mid-season trade for Baron Davis, a high-scoring point guard and superb floor general previously with the New Orleans Hornets. The Warriors missed the playoffs again, but with Davis, they caught fire over the season's final 18 games, going 14–4. "The thing I love about Baron is he delivers the ball on time," said new Golden State head coach Mike Montgomery. "You don't have to wait, you don't have to reach. The ball is delivered on time, and it's delivered to you. He's a true point guard."

The Warriors rode that momentum into the 2005–06 season, getting off to an 11–6 start in the season's first month. However, their luck didn't last. An injury to Davis sent the team into a tailspin late in the year, and Golden State plummeted to last place in the Western Conference's Pacific Division with a 34–48 mark. Montgomery was then dismissed as head coach, and the Warriors brought back Don Nelson as their bench leader.

At a stout 6-foot-3 and 215 pounds, Baron Davis was an unusually strong point guard with a knack for muscling his way to the rim.

It looked to be more of the same as Golden State stumbled at the start of the 2006–07 campaign. But in a bold, eight-player swap with the Indiana Pacers, the Warriors received a solid all-around threat in forward Al Harrington and a dangerous outside marksman in forward Stephen Jackson. These new additions, along with the greatly improved play of second-year guard Monta Ellis, sparked the Warriors. Coach Nelson created an up-tempo offense that took advantage of his young players' athleticism and created a fast-paced game that would exhaust opponents. The speedy Warriors finished with a 42–40 record and made the playoffs as the Western Conference's eighth-seeded team.

The Warriors were matched up against the 67–15 Dallas Mavericks in the first round. Despite the difference in records, the underdog Warriors stifled Dallas's star forward, Dirk Nowitzki, and toppled the Mavericks four games to two in one of the NBA's biggest playoff upsets of all time. "I don't know when I have to pinch myself or wake up from this dream," Richardson said. "This is everything I wanted. I wanted this for our fans, for our organization, for ourselves. We work hard, and we deserve it." The

dream was short-lived, as Golden State fell in round two to a physical Jazz team, dropping the series four games to one.

In the off-season, the Warriors traded Richardson and their second-round pick in the NBA Draft to Charlotte for the rights to the Bobcats' first-round pick, forward Brandan Wright. With Davis, Ellis, Jackson, Harrington, and center Andris Biedrins on the floor, and with Wright coming off the bench in a supporting role, Coach Nelson had a talented nucleus at his command.

The Warriors kept up their run-and-gun style of offense in 2007–08, raining scores of three-point shots to become the highest-scoring team in the league. Davis enjoyed one of his best seasons as a pro, netting

COURTSIDE STORIES

Guard Jason Richardson in Golden State's "The City" uniform.

RETRO COOL UNIFORMS

FROM THE 1950S TO TODAY, THE NBA HAS SEEN A VARIETY OF FASHIONS COME AND GO. Since the year 2000, the NBA has embraced "retro" uniforms—an updated fit of an old style. The Warriors' "The City" uniforms were worn for the first time in 1962 and worn again in 2004–05 when the league introduced "Hardwood Classics" nights—games in which teams through-

out the league would don retro uniforms as a tribute to the NBA's heritage. The simple blue-and-gold jerseys with the Golden Gate Bridge and the words "The City" on the front and a cable car on the back originally debuted in 1962 against the Knicks in New York. Warriors players were nervous about showcasing their new threads in the metropolis known to many as "The City,"

but the East Coast fans appreciated them. Guard Al Attles recalled, "Nobody wanted to be the first to take the [warm-up] jacket off. Finally, we take the jackets off, and I'll be darned if we don't get a stand-ing ovation from the New York crowd." *Gentleman's Quarterly* magazine ranked "The City" jersey the seventh-sharpest sports uniform of all time.

21.8 points and dishing out 7.6 assists per game. Still, it was a bitter-sweet season for the Warriors, as their 48–34 record was not quite enough to earn an invitation to the postseason.

The Warriors then made a controversial move, allowing Davis to leave town to join the Los Angeles Clippers and bringing in former Clippers swingman Corey Maggette. Injuries, inexperience, and a leaky defense kept the Warriors from realizing their potential during the 2008–09 season, and they won a mere 29 games. Although the team fared no better in 2009–10, its rebuilding efforts continued. Jackson was traded away, but picking up the slack was Stephen Curry, a baby-faced rookie guard with a sweet shooting touch. With a young roster featuring such up-and-coming talent as Ellis, Curry, and forward Anthony Randolph, and with one of the most experienced coaches in the NBA, the Warriors had designs on a resurgence in 2010–11.

COURTSIDE STORIES

RUNNING DOWN THE MAVERICKS

Guards Baron Davis (left) and Matt Barnes celebrate their 2007 upset.

IT'S ALWAYS HANDY TO HAVE AN ACE UP YOUR SLEEVE. When the eighth-seeded Warriors matched up against the top-seeded Mavericks in the first round of the 2007 playoffs, no one figured they had a ghost of a chance. What most people forgot was the Warriors' ace. Don Nelson, the Warriors' coach, had been the Mavericks' coach just two years prior, and he knew Dallas's strengths and weaknesses. The Warriors started a small lineup that was fast and very aggressive. The bigger Mavericks couldn't keep up with them when Golden State had the ball and couldn't get away from their pesky defense on the other end of the court. Point guard Baron Davis led the way for the Warriors, averaging 25 points per game in the series. The Warriors out-hustled and outsmarted the Mavericks to win the series four games to two, completing what many consider to be the NBA's biggest postseason upset since the Warriors beat the Bullets in 1975. "We made NBA history tonight," said Davis, "and that's the best thing about it. We did it as a team."

T he Warriors are one of the oldest teams in the NBA, and they are a club with a proud heritage. From their early days in Philadelphia to the modern era in the Golden State, and from greats such as Wilt Chamberlain to hardwood heroes such as Baron Davis, the Warriors have given their fans—on both coasts—decades of thrills. Now, as they enter their sixth decade of play in California, the Warriors are looking to strike championship gold yet again.

Although Golden State struggled in 2009–10, the Warriors faithful were treated to some superb offensive performances by brawny swingman Corey Maggette (below) and dynamic rookie Stephen Curry (opposite).

INDEX